Christ with me

Always

Never ending

Comfort and courage

Everlasting

Reassurance
rebirth
rest
rejoicement

Haiku Poems   for Mrs. Garrison
from Mrs. Garcia (Martin and Marina's) mom

CANCER

5   Horrible Illness
7   Not that at all, but rather
5   Christ with me always

CANCER

5   Special Encounter
7   with Jesus Christ, Son of
     GOD
5   HE chose me ... Amen

Our love and prayers
are with you and your family
Keep that positive spirit
                Garcia Family

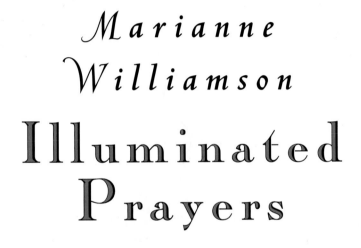

Marianne Williamson

Illuminated Prayers

Watercolors
by Claudia Karabaic Sargent

K>K
KONECKY&KONECKY

Konecky & Konecky
72 Ayers Point Rd.
Old Saybrook, CT 06475

Designed by Karolina Harris

This edition published by special arrangement
with Simon & Schuster, Inc.

ISBN: 1-56852-580-X

Printed and bound in Hong Kong

I hope *Illuminated Prayers* will be a comforting companion for those who read it. Many times my spirits have been lifted by something I found in a small spiritual volume, something I could throw in my purse and then count on to bring me back to serenity as I sat in a doctor's waiting room, stood in line at the DMV, or sat up in bed at the end of a long day. I think of prayer as a spiritual lifeline back to where I most want to be.

With that in mind, I send these prayers out into the world. I hope that they provide some solace and happiness to those who read them and utter them and feel them. They did that for me as I wrote them.

Marianne Williamson

Illuminated
Prayers

DEAR GOD,

As I wake up this morning
may Your spirit come upon me.
May my mind receive
Your emanations,
my soul receive
Your blessing,
and my heart receive
Your love.
May all those I meet

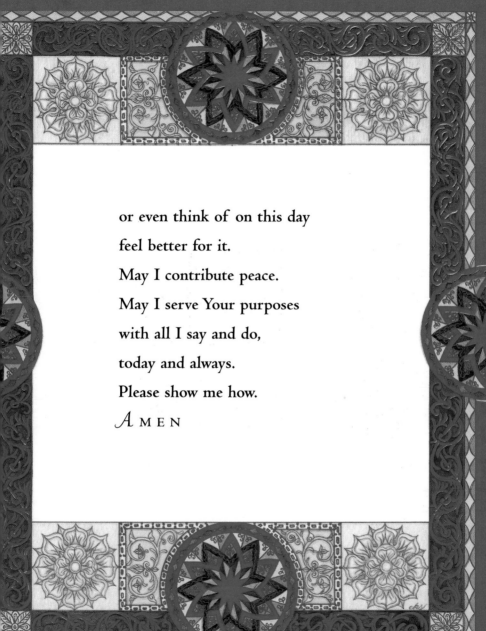

or even think of on this day
feel better for it.
May I contribute peace.
May I serve Your purposes
with all I say and do,
today and always.
Please show me how.
$\mathcal{A}$ M E N

D EAR G OD ,

here my body is broken,
please heal it.
May every cell
be filled with grace
and returned to its
divine right placement,
in me
and in all others.
A MEN

DEAR GOD,

ay my body be
a temple to Your spirit.
May every cell
be filled with light,
the radiance
of You.

May my mouth speak
only
what You would have me say.
May my legs walk
only
in the directions You would will.

May my hands
carry forth Your work
in all I say
and do.

May health be mine.
May all disease
depart
from me
and everyone.

In the name of God,
may the forces of sickness
leave
the bodies of His children,
never to return.

A M E N

DEAR GOD,

y body is broken,

I need Your help.

I fear I will not get well.

Please God,

send angels to deliver me from my pain

and sickness

and fear,

now.

I know salvation is the only true Cure,
and yet I doubt
when my body hurts.
Help me, Lord.
Please bless my medicine
and guide my healers.
Thank you, God.
$\mathcal{A}$ M E N

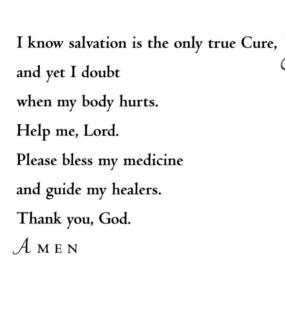

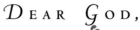

DEAR GOD,

lease send to me
the spirit of Your peace.
Then send,
dear Lord,
the spirit of peace
from me
to all the world.

May everyone I think of
and all who think of me
see only innocence
and love—

for that is who
we are.

Bless,
dear God,
my bond with others.
Make holy my relationships
and peaceful
our communications,
body to body
and
soul to soul.
A M E N

DEAR GOD,

 call to mind the people who
I saw today,
and thought of today,
and will meet tomorrow.

I surrender them to You.

Please bless each one,

and gladden each one,

and heal each one.

$\mathcal{A}$ M E N

DEAR GOD,

hen I perceive
my brothers' faults,
please transform my perceptions.
May I see only innocence,
for that is where You are.

When I am tempted
to forget
the truth
of who my sister is,

may I see only innocence,

for that is who You are.

When I am tempted to forget

that I am only love—

may I see only innocence,

for that is what You are.

$\mathcal{A}$ M E N

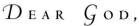

Dear God,

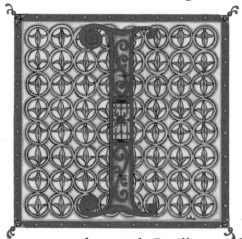 call to mind
the people I will see today.
Please bless them all.

May everyone in the world
find peace today—
each and every man
each and every woman
each and every child—
may all of them be blessed.

May the world
retrieve its purpose,
the divinity of its mission,
to reflect and glorify
Your love
forever.

$\mathcal{A}$ M E N

 D EAR G OD ,

 lease bless this marriage.

May the presence of

the Holy Spirit

come upon us

and sweetly crown our union.

May he see in me,

and I see in him,

the mystery of Heaven.
May our joys be deep
and our wounds be sacred.
Post angels to protect us, Lord,
from the demons that would
divide our hearts.
Now and forever.
A M E N

DEAR GOD,

lease break the

unhealthy bond

which keeps me tied

where I should not be tied.

Separate who should be separate,

Lord,

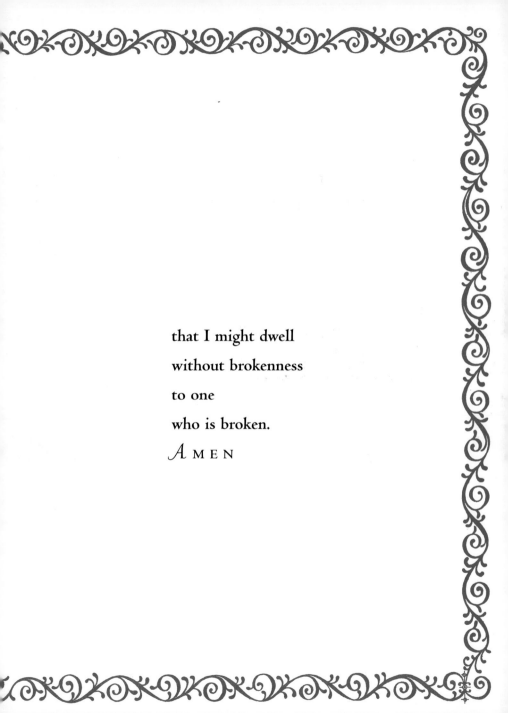

that I might dwell

without brokenness

to one

who is broken.

$\mathcal{A}$ M E N

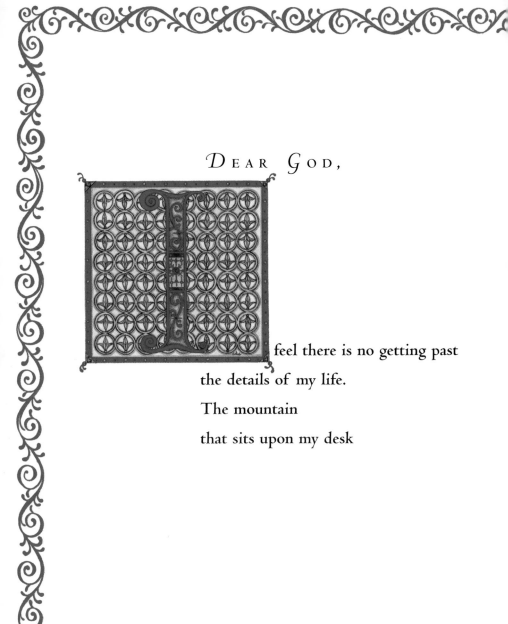

DEAR GOD,

 feel there is no getting past
the details of my life.
The mountain
that sits upon my desk

now sits

upon my heart.

Clean both,

dear God.

$\mathcal{A}$ M E N

DEAR GOD,

ay the gap which separates

earth from Heaven

close.

I surrender

my focus

on my brother's guilt,

my focus on his errors,

my instinct to condemn.

ear God,

please teach me

forgiveness.

Release us both from hell.

𝒜 M E N

DEAR GOD,

May the walls
which keep me separate—
from my brothers,
my sisters,
my self,
and You—
now melt.

May the thoughts
and feelings
which keep me in hell,
be dissolved
forever.
$\mathcal{A}$ M E N

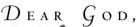

D E A R G O D ,

he world is so unsure,

I know not where to find

the safety that I seek.

I fear

when I observe the horrors

and the violence of the world.

I pray for those

now caught in it—

I pray that I might never be—

I pray for all the children,

that the darkness

coming at the world

might be turned back
and sent away
to the nothingness
from whence it came.
Lord grant me power,
that I might command the darkness—
in the name of God,
and the Holy Spirit—

 o now,
we say,
to violence
and evil
and all variety
of darkness,
go away from earth,

disembark our planet,
leave our minds
and abandon our streets,

for we claim them all

for God,

for love,

for peace.

I command you now,

in the name of God,

get away from our children,

get out of our hearts,

and do not return.

For we proclaim

the name of God,

and claim this planet for the

forces of His love.

A M E N

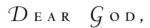

DEAR GOD,

lease bless
the children of earth,
mine and all others,
the precious angels in our midst.
Send all darkness away from them.
Thank you, God.

AMEN

DEAR GOD,

Please bless my relationship
with my (beloved)
  (friend)
  (parent)
  (child)
  (———)
Please visit
and restore us.

Please bring us both

to peace.

Melt down the walls between us,

and free us from the limits

that the walls

imposed upon us.

 less us both.

$\mathcal{A}$ M E N

Dᴇᴀʀ Gᴏᴅ,

May there come
over the earth
a great and glorious
light.

May we remember   eaven.

May all who suffer
feel pain no more.
May sorrow depart,
may disease end,
may war stop,
may doubts cease,

and all hearts
gladden.
May we remember  eaven.

May every child
and every man
and every woman
now, this instant,
feel sure release
from the bondage of their past.
$\mathcal{A}$ M E N

DEAR GOD,

lease send miracles
to the war zones
of the world.
AMEN

*D*EAR *G*OD,

Please help the children
of this world.

hey are hurt and hurting
and are crushed beneath the weight
of our insanity.
Please bless the children,
and awaken us
before it is too late.

*A*MEN

D ear G od,

Please bless the sapphire globe

and the diamonds on the water.

Please cleanse the ground

and heal the air,

and save them all from us.

orgive us

our trespasses

and make not the earth

trespass on us

as we have so trespassed

on her.

48

ave mercy on us,

and on her,

and heal our broken bond.

𝒜 M E N

D EAR G OD ,

ay miracles

replace war,

May miracles

replace hatred,

May miracles

replace judgment,

May miracles
replace fear,
in me
and in the world.
$\mathcal{A}$ M E N

DEAR GOD,

ay the sky be cleansed
May the waters be cleansed
May the ground be cleansed

May our hearts be cleansed
May our minds be cleansed
and thus made new.
A M E N

D EAR G OD ,

ay the world transform
as in a blazing fire,
and I,
oh Lord,
along with it.

A MEN

D EAR G OD,

 give to you this morning.

Please break the chain

with yesterday

and free my life to greater things.

A MEN

DEAR GOD,

lease bless our home,

the earth

wherein we dwell.

There are those who suffer here,

and know not what to do.

There are those who fear their lot,

and know not where to go.

 eal them all,
dear God,
and bring them out of darkness
into light.
A M E N

DEAR GOD,

 give to you this night.

Post angels round my home,

my bed,

my children,

my loves,

and everyone.

Send angels through the world tonight,

to heal the sick

and awaken the dead.

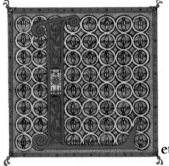et miracles
replace the pain
in all of us.
Lay Your hands on all our eyes,
that we might see
at last.

$\mathcal{A}$ M E N

DEAR GOD,

ay all the changes that would shift
this world

away from sorrow and into peace

away from violence

and into love

away from darkness and into light

now happen.

Now, not later,

now.

May a great and glorious light

emerge

and show us all

the way.

May our eyes look up at an illumined sky

and see a sign

that means

have hope

and pray,

for the Lord has found His way to you.

ow, not later,

now.

May every tear be wiped away
and every heart begin to gladden
and every life be healed by love.
Now, not later,
now.

e pray
and say thanks,
for we are heard.
He hears us.
Now, not later,
now.

$\mathcal{A}$ MEN

$\mathcal{D}$ EAR $\mathcal{G}$ OD,

ay every aspect of my being
be converted into Truth.
May every cell fall into place
and serve a higher plan.
I no longer wish to be
who I was.
 wish for more.
$\mathcal{A}$ MEN

DEAR GOD,

ay my heart
become my only perceiver
and my eyes be full of light.

May angels' wings
be lent to me,
that I might fly
above the noise
and turmoil
of the world.

ith every moment's flight
may something beautiful
be revealed to me,
and become a part
of who I am.
$\mathcal{A}$ M E N

D EAR G OD,
May the diamond center
of my love
shine forth
to magnify
Your light.

May my love
not be hidden
from me

or from others.

May You

come forth

in who I am

that

I am.

$\mathcal{A}$ M E N

DEAR GOD,

The world is like a veil

across my eyes.

I cannot see.

Please remove the veil, dear God,

and let me see beyond it.

Deliver me to peace.

 emove the scales that hide from me

the love

in every thing.

$\mathcal{A}$ MEN

D EAR G OD,

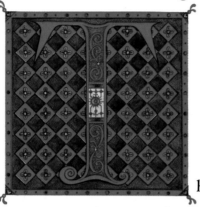

here are places in me
where I am broken.
Please touch my heart
and heal me.
Thank you, God.
A MEN

DEAR GOD,

ay all my ideas be of You.

May all my perceptions be of You.

May all my feelings be of You.

And You alone.

AMEN

Dear God,

lease make of my life
what You would have it be.
Time and fate
have twisted things
I cannot straighten out
alone.
Dear God,
may I begin again.

My body

my mind

my spirit

my love

my hate

my pain

my sorrows

my joy

my questions

my fears

my hopes

my visions

I give them all

to You.

$\mathcal{A}$ M E N

DEAR GOD,

 f it is Your will,

may I please have

the happiness I dream of.

All of it,

according to Your will,

now and forever.

Thank you, God.

AMEN

DEAR GOD,

 cannot describe in words
the misery I feel.
But you know.
Please enter my heart
transform my thoughts
make straight my way
and set me free.
Thank you, God.
AMEN

DEAR GOD,

lease help me.
I can sense the beauty of Heaven
and the peace of Your arms,
but I cannot find them
here.
May I come home while still on earth?
Please take me there, and keep me.
Thank you, God.

AMEN

D EAR G OD,

ay my gifts
begin to blossom
in a way that serves Your plan.
A MEN

DEAR GOD,

lease lift the veil
that separates me
from the Heaven which lay beyond.
Renew my thoughts
so full of fear and judgment and the illusions
  of the world
Renew my heart
so burdened by the sorrows of the past
Renew my hopes

o often squelched.

send angels, God,

to sit with me and walk with me

and whisper in my ears.

May I be

here for You

and here with You

and see You in all things.

Please help me see the innocence of life.

A M E N

DEAR GOD,

his season,
may I be reborn
washed clean
made new
forgiven
spectacularly loved.

emind me who I am.

Forgive me for my shadow sides,

please heal my broken wings

that I might fly

with You.

A M E N

DEAR GOD,

ay all the tears I cry, and all the

tears

I have not cried

but hold within,

pour forth into Your hands.

Please take each painful thought
and unhealed wound,
and send Your angels
here
to me.
I long for peace.
$\mathcal{A}$ M E N

DEAR GOD,

lease sew my heart back together.

AMEN

DEAR GOD,

he memories that haunt
me now
please take away
forever.
AMEN

Dear God,

lease forgive me my
errors.

I surrender now
my shame,
my guilt,
the wrongs which I have done.
I am so sorry.
I atone.

I go back,
dear Lord,

to the moment of disruption.

I give to You

that moment.

Please give new life

to me.

orgive me,

and teach me how to forgive

myself

and others.

$\mathcal{A}$ MEN

D EAR G OD,

ay hatred be forever
banished
from the universe.
In the name of God,
may hatred cease.
Make my heart a harmless,
peaceful place.
A MEN

D EAR G OD,
May the stars
which fill the sky
fill me.
A MEN

DEAR GOD,
May I cross over now
from boy to man,
(from girl to woman)
from child to adult
at last.
AMEN

DEAR GOD,

hen they accuse me falsely,
help them see the innocence in me.
And when I judge, Lord,
help me see the innocence in them.
AMEN

*D*EAR *G*OD,
Please help me dedicate
myself to You—
to do the work,
to quiet my mind,
that I might serve You best.

Please introduce my heart
to peace,
and guide me to the chamber
where my heart
can rest
and find itself.
Please take me there.

$\mathcal{A}$ M E N

DEAR GOD,

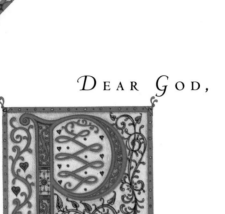

lease take from me

the burdens I carry,

and answer

the questions that haunt me.

Please reveal to me

the purpose of my life,

the reasons for my pain,

and the mystery of Your plan.

AMEN

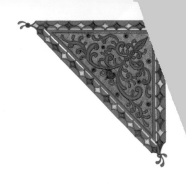

$\mathcal{D}$ E A R $\mathcal{G}$ O D ,

Please take away
my inappropriate
desires.
Please release me
from my cravings.

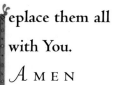

eplace them all
with You.
$\mathcal{A}$ M E N

DEAR GOD,

lease help me to detach
from things that hold me back.
Remove from me
illusions and falsehood.
Restore to me
the lightness
of my being.
AMEN

DEAR GOD,

lease bless the ones
who have no hope,
and show me how to help.
AMEN

*D*EAR *G*OD,

lease bless my mother and
father
my teachers and healers
my friends and lovers
my children and theirs.
*A*MEN

D<small>EAR</small> G<small>OD</small>,

Please mend my broken relationships
for I do not know how.

how me their innocence
and please show them mine.

Thank you, Lord.

A<small>MEN</small>

Dear God,

Please bless my country
and every country.
Forgive this century
its violence and pain,
and bless the century now upon us.

Amen

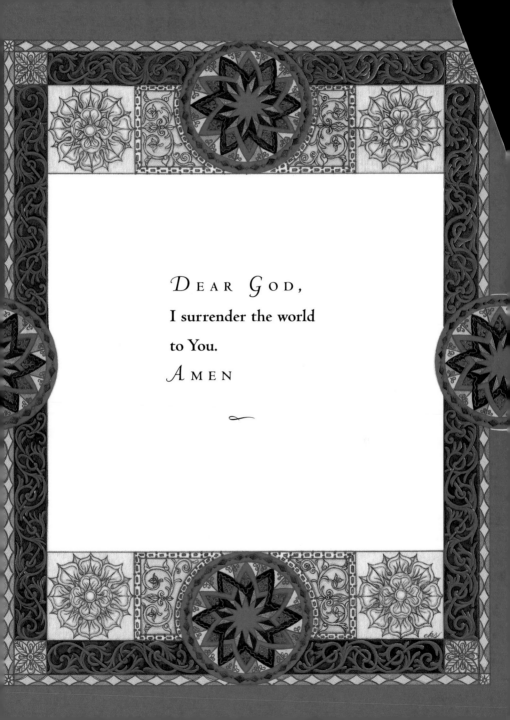

DEAR GOD,
I surrender the world
to You.
AMEN

About the Author

Marianne Williamson is the best-selling author of *A Return to Love, A Woman's Worth, Illuminata,* and *The Healing of America.* She is also the author of a children's book, *Emma and Mommy Talk to God.*